50 Decadent Vanilla Cake Layer Recipes

By: Kelly Johnson

Table of Contents

- Classic Vanilla Buttercream Cake
- Vanilla Bean and Almond Layer Cake
- Vanilla and Chocolate Fudge Layer Cake
- Vanilla Chiffon Cake
- Vanilla Bean Cheesecake Cake
- Vanilla Raspberry Jam Layer Cake
- Vanilla Coconut Cream Cake
- Vanilla Lemon Cream Layer Cake
- White Chocolate Vanilla Cake
- Vanilla Hazelnut Crunch Cake
- Vanilla Pecan Layer Cake
- Vanilla Caramel Swirl Cake
- Vanilla Mocha Cake
- Vanilla Strawberry Shortcake Cake
- Vanilla Matcha Layer Cake
- Vanilla Bean and Peach Cake
- Vanilla Cream Cheese Layer Cake
- Vanilla Cinnamon Roll Layer Cake
- Vanilla Almond and Cherry Cake
- Vanilla Coconut Meringue Cake
- Vanilla Blueberry Swirl Cake
- Vanilla and Maple Pecan Cake
- Vanilla Cream Puffs Cake
- Vanilla Tiramisu Layer Cake
- Vanilla and Dark Chocolate Ganache Cake
- Vanilla and Lemon Meringue Cake
- Vanilla Raspberry Rose Cake
- Vanilla Hazelnut Truffle Cake
- Vanilla Orange Blossom Cake
- Vanilla Mint Buttercream Cake
- Vanilla Pistachio Layer Cake
- Vanilla Lemon Poppy Seed Cake
- Vanilla Fudge Marble Cake
- Vanilla Red Velvet Cake
- Vanilla Buttercream and Fruit Tart Cake

- Vanilla Toffee Crunch Cake
- Vanilla with Caramelized Banana Cake
- Vanilla and White Chocolate Truffle Cake
- Vanilla Maple Bacon Cake
- Vanilla and Cherry Cheesecake Cake
- Vanilla Sugar Cookie Layer Cake
- Vanilla Cream and Raspberry Mousse Cake
- Vanilla Mint Chocolate Chip Cake
- Vanilla Cream Puff Swirl Cake
- Vanilla Fig and Almond Cake
- Vanilla Pineapple Coconut Cake
- Vanilla Blackberry Jam Cake
- Vanilla Custard Layer Cake
- Vanilla Maple Pecan Layer Cake
- Vanilla and Coffee Bean Layer Cake

Classic Vanilla Buttercream Cake

Ingredients

For the Cake:

- 2 ½ cups (310g) all-purpose flour
- 1 ½ tsp baking powder
- ¼ tsp salt
- 1 cup (230g) unsalted butter, softened
- 1 ½ cups (300g) granulated sugar
- 3 large eggs
- 1 tsp vanilla extract
- 1 cup (240ml) milk

For the Buttercream Frosting:

- 1 cup (230g) unsalted butter, softened
- 4 cups (480g) powdered sugar
- 1 tsp vanilla extract
- 2 tbsp heavy cream
- Pinch of salt

Instructions

1. **Prepare the Cake:**
    - Preheat the oven to 350°F (175°C). Grease and line two 9-inch (23cm) round cake pans.
    - In a bowl, whisk together flour, baking powder, and salt.
    - In a large bowl, beat the butter and sugar until light and fluffy. Add eggs one at a time, mixing well after each addition. Stir in vanilla extract.
    - Gradually add the dry ingredients alternating with milk, mixing until smooth.
    - Divide the batter between the pans and bake for 25–30 minutes or until a toothpick comes out clean. Let the cakes cool completely.
2. **Prepare the Buttercream Frosting:**
    - Beat the butter until smooth and creamy. Gradually add powdered sugar, beating until fluffy. Add vanilla, heavy cream, and a pinch of salt. Beat until smooth and light.
3. **Assemble the Cake:**
    - Frost the cooled cakes with vanilla buttercream. Decorate as desired.

Vanilla Bean and Almond Layer Cake

Ingredients

For the Cake:

- 2 ½ cups (310g) all-purpose flour
- 1 ½ tsp baking powder
- ¼ tsp salt
- 1 cup (230g) unsalted butter, softened
- 1 ½ cups (300g) granulated sugar
- 3 large eggs
- 1 tsp vanilla extract
- 1 tsp almond extract
- 1 cup (240ml) milk
- 1 vanilla bean, split and scraped

For the Frosting:

- 2 cups (480ml) heavy whipping cream
- 1 tsp almond extract
- ½ cup (50g) powdered sugar

Instructions

1. **Prepare the Cake:**
    - Preheat the oven to 350°F (175°C). Grease and line two 9-inch (23cm) round cake pans.
    - In a bowl, whisk together flour, baking powder, and salt.
    - In a large bowl, beat the butter and sugar until light and fluffy. Add eggs one at a time, mixing well after each addition. Stir in vanilla extract, almond extract, and scraped vanilla bean.
    - Gradually add the dry ingredients alternating with milk, mixing until smooth.
    - Divide the batter between the pans and bake for 25–30 minutes or until a toothpick comes out clean. Let the cakes cool completely.
2. **Prepare the Frosting:**
    - Whip the heavy cream with powdered sugar and almond extract until stiff peaks form.
3. **Assemble the Cake:**

- Frost the cooled cakes with almond-infused whipped cream and decorate with extra vanilla bean seeds.

Vanilla and Chocolate Fudge Layer Cake

Ingredients

For the Vanilla Cake:

- 2 ½ cups (310g) all-purpose flour
- 1 ½ tsp baking powder
- ¼ tsp salt
- 1 cup (230g) unsalted butter, softened
- 1 ½ cups (300g) granulated sugar
- 3 large eggs
- 1 tsp vanilla extract
- 1 cup (240ml) milk

For the Chocolate Fudge Cake:

- 1 ¾ cups (220g) all-purpose flour
- 1 ½ cups (300g) granulated sugar
- ½ cup (50g) unsweetened cocoa powder
- 1 ½ tsp baking soda
- 1 tsp baking powder
- ¼ tsp salt
- 1 cup (240ml) boiling water
- 1 cup (230g) unsalted butter, softened
- 2 large eggs
- 1 tsp vanilla extract

For the Frosting:

- 2 cups (480ml) heavy whipping cream
- 8 oz (225g) semi-sweet chocolate, chopped
- ½ cup (100g) granulated sugar
- 2 tsp vanilla extract

Instructions

1. **Prepare the Vanilla Cake:**
    - Preheat the oven to 350°F (175°C). Grease and line two 9-inch (23cm) round cake pans.
    - In a bowl, whisk together flour, baking powder, and salt.

- In a large bowl, beat the butter and sugar until light and fluffy. Add eggs one at a time, mixing well after each addition. Stir in vanilla extract.
- Gradually add the dry ingredients alternating with milk, mixing until smooth.
- Divide the batter between the pans and bake for 25–30 minutes or until a toothpick comes out clean. Let the cakes cool completely.

2. **Prepare the Chocolate Fudge Cake:**
   - Preheat the oven to 350°F (175°C). Grease and line two 9-inch (23cm) round cake pans.
   - In a bowl, whisk together flour, sugar, cocoa powder, baking soda, baking powder, and salt.
   - In a separate bowl, whisk together the boiling water, butter, eggs, and vanilla. Add to the dry ingredients and mix until smooth.
   - Divide the batter between the pans and bake for 30–35 minutes or until a toothpick comes out clean. Let the cakes cool completely.

3. **Prepare the Frosting:**
   - Heat heavy cream in a saucepan until simmering. Pour over chopped chocolate and stir until smooth. Stir in sugar and vanilla extract. Let it cool.

4. **Assemble the Cake:**
   - Layer the vanilla and chocolate fudge cakes, alternating between them. Frost with chocolate whipped cream and decorate as desired.

Vanilla Chiffon Cake

Ingredients

For the Cake:

- 2 ½ cups (310g) all-purpose flour
- 1 ½ tsp baking powder
- ¼ tsp salt
- 1 cup (230g) granulated sugar
- 1 tsp vanilla extract
- 6 large eggs, separated
- 1 cup (240ml) vegetable oil
- 1 cup (240ml) water

For the Frosting:

- 1 cup (240ml) heavy whipping cream
- ½ cup (50g) powdered sugar
- 1 tsp vanilla extract

Instructions

1. **Prepare the Cake:**
    - Preheat the oven to 325°F (165°C). Grease and line a 10-inch tube pan.
    - In a bowl, whisk together flour, baking powder, salt, and sugar.
    - In a large bowl, combine egg yolks, oil, vanilla, and water. Add the dry ingredients and mix until smooth.
    - In a separate bowl, beat egg whites until stiff peaks form. Gently fold the egg whites into the batter.
    - Pour the batter into the prepared pan and bake for 45–50 minutes or until a toothpick comes out clean. Let the cake cool upside down.
2. **Prepare the Frosting:**
    - Whip the heavy cream with powdered sugar and vanilla extract until stiff peaks form.
3. **Assemble the Cake:**
    - Frost the cooled chiffon cake with whipped cream and decorate as desired.

Vanilla Bean Cheesecake Cake

Ingredients

For the Cheesecake Layer:

- 1 ½ cups (360g) cream cheese, softened
- ¾ cup (150g) granulated sugar
- 2 large eggs
- 1 tsp vanilla extract
- 1 ½ cups (360ml) heavy cream

For the Cake:

- 2 ½ cups (310g) all-purpose flour
- 1 ½ tsp baking powder
- ¼ tsp salt
- 1 cup (230g) unsalted butter, softened
- 1 ½ cups (300g) granulated sugar
- 3 large eggs
- 1 tsp vanilla extract
- 1 cup (240ml) milk
- 1 vanilla bean, split and scraped

For the Frosting:

- 2 cups (480ml) heavy whipping cream
- 1 cup (120g) powdered sugar
- 1 tsp vanilla extract

Instructions

1. **Prepare the Cheesecake Layer:**
    - Preheat the oven to 325°F (165°C). Grease and line a 9-inch (23cm) round cake pan.
    - Beat cream cheese and sugar until smooth. Add eggs one at a time, mixing well. Stir in vanilla extract.
    - Pour mixture into the pan and bake for 30–35 minutes or until set. Let it cool.
2. **Prepare the Cake:**

    - Preheat the oven to 350°F (175°C). Grease and line two 9-inch (23cm) round cake pans.
    - In a bowl, whisk together flour, baking powder, and salt.
    - In a large bowl, beat the butter and sugar until light and fluffy. Add eggs one at a time, mixing well. Stir in vanilla and scraped vanilla bean.
    - Gradually add the dry ingredients alternating with milk, mixing until smooth.
    - Divide the batter between the pans and bake for 25–30 minutes or until a toothpick comes out clean. Let the cakes cool completely.
3. **Prepare the Frosting:**
    - Whip the heavy cream with powdered sugar and vanilla extract until stiff peaks form.
4. **Assemble the Cake:**
    - Layer the cheesecake layer between the two cakes. Frost the top and sides with whipped cream. Decorate as desired.

Vanilla Hazelnut Crunch Cake

Ingredients

For the Cake:

- 2 ½ cups (310g) all-purpose flour
- 1 ½ tsp baking powder
- ¼ tsp salt
- 1 cup (230g) unsalted butter, softened
- 1 ½ cups (300g) granulated sugar
- 3 large eggs
- 1 tsp vanilla extract
- 1 cup (240ml) milk
- 1 cup (120g) hazelnuts, chopped and toasted

For the Hazelnut Crunch:

- 1 cup (120g) hazelnuts, chopped
- ¼ cup (50g) granulated sugar
- ¼ cup (60ml) heavy cream

For the Frosting:

- 2 cups (480ml) heavy whipping cream
- 1 cup (120g) powdered sugar
- 1 tsp vanilla extract

Instructions

1. **Prepare the Cake:**
   - Preheat the oven to 350°F (175°C). Grease and line two 9-inch (23cm) round cake pans.
   - In a bowl, whisk together flour, baking powder, and salt.
   - In a large bowl, beat the butter and sugar until light and fluffy. Add eggs one at a time, mixing well after each addition. Stir in vanilla extract.
   - Gradually add the dry ingredients alternating with milk, mixing until smooth. Fold in the chopped toasted hazelnuts.
   - Divide the batter between the pans and bake for 25–30 minutes or until a toothpick comes out clean. Let the cakes cool completely.
2. **Prepare the Hazelnut Crunch:**

- In a small saucepan, heat the sugar and heavy cream over medium heat, stirring until the sugar dissolves and the mixture comes to a simmer. Stir in the chopped hazelnuts and cook for 2–3 minutes until the syrup thickens. Remove from heat and allow to cool.
3. **Prepare the Frosting:**
    - Whip the heavy cream with powdered sugar and vanilla extract until stiff peaks form.
4. **Assemble the Cake:**
    - Layer the cakes and spread frosting between each layer. Top with the hazelnut crunch and serve.

Vanilla Pecan Layer Cake

Ingredients

For the Cake:

- 2 ½ cups (310g) all-purpose flour
- 1 ½ tsp baking powder
- ¼ tsp salt
- 1 cup (230g) unsalted butter, softened
- 1 ½ cups (300g) granulated sugar
- 3 large eggs
- 1 tsp vanilla extract
- 1 cup (240ml) milk
- 1 cup (120g) chopped pecans, toasted

For the Frosting:

- 2 cups (480ml) heavy whipping cream
- ½ cup (60g) powdered sugar
- 1 tsp vanilla extract
- 1 cup (120g) chopped toasted pecans

Instructions

1. **Prepare the Cake:**
    - Preheat the oven to 350°F (175°C). Grease and line two 9-inch (23cm) round cake pans.
    - In a bowl, whisk together flour, baking powder, and salt.
    - In a large bowl, beat the butter and sugar until light and fluffy. Add eggs one at a time, mixing well. Stir in vanilla extract.
    - Gradually add the dry ingredients alternating with milk, mixing until smooth. Fold in the chopped pecans.
    - Divide the batter between the pans and bake for 25–30 minutes or until a toothpick comes out clean. Let the cakes cool completely.
2. **Prepare the Frosting:**
    - Whip the heavy cream with powdered sugar and vanilla extract until stiff peaks form.
3. **Assemble the Cake:**
    - Layer the cakes and frost with whipped cream. Sprinkle with toasted pecans between layers and on top.

Vanilla Caramel Swirl Cake

Ingredients

For the Cake:

- 2 ½ cups (310g) all-purpose flour
- 1 ½ tsp baking powder
- ¼ tsp salt
- 1 cup (230g) unsalted butter, softened
- 1 ½ cups (300g) granulated sugar
- 3 large eggs
- 1 tsp vanilla extract
- 1 cup (240ml) milk
- ½ cup (120ml) caramel sauce, divided

For the Frosting:

- 2 cups (480ml) heavy whipping cream
- ½ cup (50g) powdered sugar
- 1 tsp vanilla extract
- ½ cup (120ml) caramel sauce

Instructions

1. **Prepare the Cake:**
     - Preheat the oven to 350°F (175°C). Grease and line two 9-inch (23cm) round cake pans.
     - In a bowl, whisk together flour, baking powder, and salt.
     - In a large bowl, beat the butter and sugar until light and fluffy. Add eggs one at a time, mixing well after each addition. Stir in vanilla extract.
     - Gradually add the dry ingredients alternating with milk, mixing until smooth. Gently swirl in half of the caramel sauce.
     - Divide the batter between the pans and bake for 25–30 minutes or until a toothpick comes out clean. Let the cakes cool completely.
2. **Prepare the Frosting:**
     - Whip the heavy cream with powdered sugar and vanilla extract until stiff peaks form. Drizzle in the remaining caramel sauce and mix.
3. **Assemble the Cake:**
     - Layer the cakes and frost with the caramel cream frosting. Drizzle extra caramel on top for decoration.

Vanilla Mocha Cake

Ingredients

For the Cake:

- 2 ½ cups (310g) all-purpose flour
- 1 ½ tsp baking powder
- ¼ tsp salt
- 1 cup (230g) unsalted butter, softened
- 1 ½ cups (300g) granulated sugar
- 3 large eggs
- 1 tsp vanilla extract
- 1 cup (240ml) milk
- ¼ cup (60ml) strong brewed coffee, cooled
- 1 tbsp cocoa powder

For the Frosting:

- 2 cups (480ml) heavy whipping cream
- ½ cup (50g) powdered sugar
- 1 tsp vanilla extract
- 2 tbsp instant coffee granules
- 1 tbsp cocoa powder

Instructions

1. **Prepare the Cake:**
   - Preheat the oven to 350°F (175°C). Grease and line two 9-inch (23cm) round cake pans.
   - In a bowl, whisk together flour, baking powder, salt, and cocoa powder.
   - In a large bowl, beat the butter and sugar until light and fluffy. Add eggs one at a time, mixing well. Stir in vanilla extract.
   - Gradually add the dry ingredients alternating with milk and brewed coffee, mixing until smooth.
   - Divide the batter between the pans and bake for 25–30 minutes or until a toothpick comes out clean. Let the cakes cool completely.
2. **Prepare the Frosting:**
   - Whip the heavy cream with powdered sugar and vanilla extract until stiff peaks form. Dissolve the instant coffee granules and cocoa powder in a little warm water and add it to the whipped cream.

3. **Assemble the Cake:**
    - Layer the cakes and frost with the mocha whipped cream. Decorate with chocolate shavings or coffee beans if desired.

Vanilla Strawberry Shortcake Cake

Ingredients

For the Cake:

- 2 ½ cups (310g) all-purpose flour
- 1 ½ tsp baking powder
- ¼ tsp salt
- 1 cup (230g) unsalted butter, softened
- 1 ½ cups (300g) granulated sugar
- 3 large eggs
- 1 tsp vanilla extract
- 1 cup (240ml) milk

For the Strawberry Filling:

- 3 cups (450g) fresh strawberries, hulled and sliced
- ¼ cup (50g) granulated sugar

For the Frosting:

- 2 cups (480ml) heavy whipping cream
- ½ cup (50g) powdered sugar
- 1 tsp vanilla extract

Instructions

1. **Prepare the Cake:**
   - Preheat the oven to 350°F (175°C). Grease and line two 9-inch (23cm) round cake pans.
   - In a bowl, whisk together flour, baking powder, and salt.
   - In a large bowl, beat the butter and sugar until light and fluffy. Add eggs one at a time, mixing well after each addition. Stir in vanilla extract.
   - Gradually add the dry ingredients alternating with milk, mixing until smooth.
   - Divide the batter between the pans and bake for 25–30 minutes or until a toothpick comes out clean. Let the cakes cool completely.
2. **Prepare the Strawberry Filling:**
   - Mix the sliced strawberries with sugar and let sit for about 10–15 minutes until the juices are released.

3. **Prepare the Frosting:**
    - Whip the heavy cream with powdered sugar and vanilla extract until stiff peaks form.
4. **Assemble the Cake:**
    - Layer the cakes, adding strawberry filling between layers. Frost the top and sides with whipped cream. Garnish with extra strawberries.

Vanilla Almond and Cherry Cake

Ingredients

For the Cake:

- 2 ½ cups (310g) all-purpose flour
- 1 ½ tsp baking powder
- ¼ tsp salt
- 1 cup (230g) unsalted butter, softened
- 1 ½ cups (300g) granulated sugar
- 3 large eggs
- 1 tsp vanilla extract
- 1 tsp almond extract
- 1 cup (240ml) milk
- 1 cup (150g) cherries, pitted and chopped
- ½ cup (50g) sliced almonds

For the Frosting:

- 2 cups (480ml) heavy whipping cream
- ½ cup (50g) powdered sugar
- 1 tsp vanilla extract

Instructions

1. **Prepare the Cake:**
    - Preheat the oven to 350°F (175°C). Grease and line two 9-inch (23cm) round cake pans.
    - In a bowl, whisk together flour, baking powder, and salt.
    - In a large bowl, beat the butter and sugar until light and fluffy. Add eggs one at a time, mixing well. Stir in vanilla and almond extracts.
    - Gradually add the dry ingredients alternating with milk, mixing until smooth. Fold in the chopped cherries and sliced almonds.
    - Divide the batter between the pans and bake for 25–30 minutes or until a toothpick comes out clean. Let the cakes cool completely.
2. **Prepare the Frosting:**
    - Whip the heavy cream with powdered sugar and vanilla extract until stiff peaks form.
3. **Assemble the Cake:**

- Layer the cakes, frosting each layer with whipped cream. Garnish with extra cherries and almonds on top.

Vanilla Coconut Meringue Cake

Ingredients

For the Cake:

- 2 ½ cups (310g) all-purpose flour
- 1 ½ tsp baking powder
- ¼ tsp salt
- 1 cup (230g) unsalted butter, softened
- 1 ½ cups (300g) granulated sugar
- 3 large eggs
- 1 tsp vanilla extract
- 1 cup (240ml) coconut milk
- 1 cup (100g) shredded coconut

For the Meringue:

- 4 large egg whites
- 1 cup (200g) granulated sugar
- 1 tsp vanilla extract

For the Frosting:

- 1 ½ cups (360ml) heavy whipping cream
- ½ cup (50g) powdered sugar
- 1 tsp vanilla extract

Instructions

1. **Prepare the Cake:**
    - Preheat the oven to 350°F (175°C). Grease and line two 9-inch (23cm) round cake pans.
    - In a bowl, whisk together flour, baking powder, and salt.
    - In a large bowl, beat the butter and sugar until light and fluffy. Add eggs one at a time, mixing well after each addition. Stir in vanilla extract.
    - Gradually add the dry ingredients alternating with coconut milk, mixing until smooth. Fold in the shredded coconut.
    - Divide the batter between the pans and bake for 25–30 minutes or until a toothpick comes out clean. Let the cakes cool completely.
2. **Prepare the Meringue:**

- Beat the egg whites until soft peaks form. Gradually add the sugar and vanilla extract, beating until stiff peaks form.
3. **Prepare the Frosting:**
    - Whip the heavy cream with powdered sugar and vanilla extract until stiff peaks form.
4. **Assemble the Cake:**
    - Layer the cakes, spreading frosting between each layer. Top the cake with meringue, gently toasting the top with a kitchen torch or placing it in the oven for a few minutes to lightly brown.

Vanilla Blueberry Swirl Cake

Ingredients

For the Cake:

- 2 ½ cups (310g) all-purpose flour
- 1 ½ tsp baking powder
- ¼ tsp salt
- 1 cup (230g) unsalted butter, softened
- 1 ½ cups (300g) granulated sugar
- 3 large eggs
- 1 tsp vanilla extract
- 1 cup (240ml) milk
- 1 cup (150g) fresh blueberries
- 1 tbsp cornstarch (for dusting the blueberries)

For the Frosting:

- 2 cups (480ml) heavy whipping cream
- ½ cup (50g) powdered sugar
- 1 tsp vanilla extract

Instructions

1. **Prepare the Cake:**
    - Preheat the oven to 350°F (175°C). Grease and line two 9-inch (23cm) round cake pans.
    - In a bowl, whisk together flour, baking powder, and salt.
    - In a large bowl, beat the butter and sugar until light and fluffy. Add eggs one at a time, mixing well after each addition. Stir in vanilla extract.
    - Gradually add the dry ingredients alternating with milk, mixing until smooth.
    - Toss the blueberries in cornstarch to prevent them from sinking, then gently fold them into the batter.
    - Divide the batter between the pans and bake for 25–30 minutes or until a toothpick comes out clean. Let the cakes cool completely.
2. **Prepare the Frosting:**
    - Whip the heavy cream with powdered sugar and vanilla extract until stiff peaks form.
3. **Assemble the Cake:**

- Layer the cakes, spreading frosting between each layer. Top the cake with more fresh blueberries.

Vanilla and Maple Pecan Cake

Ingredients

For the Cake:

- 2 ½ cups (310g) all-purpose flour
- 1 ½ tsp baking powder
- ¼ tsp salt
- 1 cup (230g) unsalted butter, softened
- 1 ½ cups (300g) granulated sugar
- 3 large eggs
- 1 tsp vanilla extract
- 1 cup (240ml) maple syrup
- 1 cup (120g) toasted pecans, chopped

For the Frosting:

- 2 cups (480ml) heavy whipping cream
- ½ cup (50g) powdered sugar
- 1 tsp vanilla extract

Instructions

1. **Prepare the Cake:**
    - Preheat the oven to 350°F (175°C). Grease and line two 9-inch (23cm) round cake pans.
    - In a bowl, whisk together flour, baking powder, and salt.
    - In a large bowl, beat the butter and sugar until light and fluffy. Add eggs one at a time, mixing well after each addition. Stir in vanilla extract and maple syrup.
    - Gradually add the dry ingredients, mixing until smooth. Fold in the toasted pecans.
    - Divide the batter between the pans and bake for 25–30 minutes or until a toothpick comes out clean. Let the cakes cool completely.
2. **Prepare the Frosting:**
    - Whip the heavy cream with powdered sugar and vanilla extract until stiff peaks form.
3. **Assemble the Cake:**
    - Layer the cakes, frosting each layer with whipped cream. Garnish with additional toasted pecans and a drizzle of maple syrup.

Vanilla Cream Puffs Cake

Ingredients

For the Cake:

- 2 ½ cups (310g) all-purpose flour
- 1 ½ tsp baking powder
- ¼ tsp salt
- 1 cup (230g) unsalted butter, softened
- 1 ½ cups (300g) granulated sugar
- 3 large eggs
- 1 tsp vanilla extract
- 1 cup (240ml) milk
- 1 cup (100g) cream puff filling (prepared ahead of time)

For the Frosting:

- 2 cups (480ml) heavy whipping cream
- ½ cup (50g) powdered sugar
- 1 tsp vanilla extract

Instructions

1. **Prepare the Cake:**
    - Preheat the oven to 350°F (175°C). Grease and line two 9-inch (23cm) round cake pans.
    - In a bowl, whisk together flour, baking powder, and salt.
    - In a large bowl, beat the butter and sugar until light and fluffy. Add eggs one at a time, mixing well after each addition. Stir in vanilla extract.
    - Gradually add the dry ingredients alternating with milk, mixing until smooth. Fold in the cream puff filling.
    - Divide the batter between the pans and bake for 25–30 minutes or until a toothpick comes out clean. Let the cakes cool completely.
2. **Prepare the Frosting:**
    - Whip the heavy cream with powdered sugar and vanilla extract until stiff peaks form.
3. **Assemble the Cake:**
    - Layer the cakes and frost with whipped cream. Add dollops of cream puff filling between the layers for extra richness.

Vanilla Hazelnut Truffle Cake

Ingredients

For the Cake:

- 2 ½ cups (310g) all-purpose flour
- 1 ½ tsp baking powder
- ¼ tsp salt
- 1 cup (230g) unsalted butter, softened
- 1 ½ cups (300g) granulated sugar
- 3 large eggs
- 1 tsp vanilla extract
- 1 cup (240ml) milk
- 1 cup (100g) toasted hazelnuts, chopped
- ½ cup (80g) dark chocolate truffle pieces, chopped

For the Frosting:

- 2 cups (480ml) heavy whipping cream
- ½ cup (50g) powdered sugar
- 1 tsp vanilla extract
- ½ cup (50g) chopped hazelnuts for garnish
- ½ cup (50g) dark chocolate ganache for drizzle

Instructions

1. **Prepare the Cake:**
    - Preheat the oven to 350°F (175°C). Grease and line two 9-inch (23cm) round cake pans.
    - In a bowl, whisk together flour, baking powder, and salt.
    - In a large bowl, beat the butter and sugar until light and fluffy. Add eggs one at a time, mixing well. Stir in vanilla extract.
    - Gradually add the dry ingredients alternating with milk, mixing until smooth. Fold in the chopped hazelnuts and dark chocolate truffle pieces.
    - Divide the batter between the pans and bake for 25–30 minutes or until a toothpick comes out clean. Let the cakes cool completely.
2. **Prepare the Frosting:**
    - Whip the heavy cream with powdered sugar and vanilla extract until stiff peaks form.
3. **Assemble the Cake:**

- Layer the cakes, spreading whipped cream frosting between each layer. Top the cake with ganache and chopped hazelnuts for garnish.

Vanilla Orange Blossom Cake

Ingredients

For the Cake:

- 2 ½ cups (310g) all-purpose flour
- 1 ½ tsp baking powder
- ¼ tsp salt
- 1 cup (230g) unsalted butter, softened
- 1 ½ cups (300g) granulated sugar
- 3 large eggs
- 1 tsp vanilla extract
- ½ tsp orange blossom water
- 1 cup (240ml) milk
- Zest of 1 orange

For the Frosting:

- 2 cups (480ml) heavy whipping cream
- ½ cup (50g) powdered sugar
- 1 tsp vanilla extract
- 1 tsp orange blossom water

Instructions

1. **Prepare the Cake:**
    - Preheat the oven to 350°F (175°C). Grease and line two 9-inch (23cm) round cake pans.
    - In a bowl, whisk together flour, baking powder, and salt.
    - In a large bowl, beat the butter and sugar until light and fluffy. Add eggs one at a time, mixing well after each. Stir in vanilla extract and orange blossom water.
    - Gradually add the dry ingredients alternating with milk, mixing until smooth. Stir in the orange zest.
    - Divide the batter between the pans and bake for 25–30 minutes or until a toothpick comes out clean. Let the cakes cool completely.
2. **Prepare the Frosting:**
    - Whip the heavy cream with powdered sugar, vanilla extract, and orange blossom water until stiff peaks form.
3. **Assemble the Cake:**

    - Layer the cakes, spreading frosting between each layer. Garnish with orange zest and edible flowers if desired.

Vanilla Mint Buttercream Cake

Ingredients

For the Cake:

- 2 ½ cups (310g) all-purpose flour
- 1 ½ tsp baking powder
- ¼ tsp salt
- 1 cup (230g) unsalted butter, softened
- 1 ½ cups (300g) granulated sugar
- 3 large eggs
- 1 tsp vanilla extract
- 1 cup (240ml) milk
- 1 tbsp fresh mint leaves, finely chopped

For the Frosting:

- 2 cups (480ml) heavy whipping cream
- ½ cup (50g) powdered sugar
- 1 tsp vanilla extract
- 2 tbsp fresh mint leaves, finely chopped
- Green food coloring (optional)

Instructions

1. **Prepare the Cake:**
    - Preheat the oven to 350°F (175°C). Grease and line two 9-inch (23cm) round cake pans.
    - In a bowl, whisk together flour, baking powder, and salt.
    - In a large bowl, beat the butter and sugar until light and fluffy. Add eggs one at a time, mixing well after each addition. Stir in vanilla extract.
    - Gradually add the dry ingredients alternating with milk, mixing until smooth. Fold in the chopped mint leaves.
    - Divide the batter between the pans and bake for 25–30 minutes or until a toothpick comes out clean. Let the cakes cool completely.
2. **Prepare the Frosting:**
    - Whip the heavy cream with powdered sugar and vanilla extract until stiff peaks form. Gently fold in the chopped mint leaves and a few drops of green food coloring if desired.
3. **Assemble the Cake:**

- Layer the cakes, spreading mint buttercream between each layer. Frost the top and sides of the cake with the remaining frosting. Garnish with fresh mint leaves.

Vanilla Pistachio Layer Cake

Ingredients

For the Cake:

- 2 ½ cups (310g) all-purpose flour
- 1 ½ tsp baking powder
- ¼ tsp salt
- 1 cup (230g) unsalted butter, softened
- 1 ½ cups (300g) granulated sugar
- 3 large eggs
- 1 tsp vanilla extract
- 1 cup (240ml) milk
- ½ cup (50g) pistachios, chopped

For the Frosting:

- 2 cups (480ml) heavy whipping cream
- ½ cup (50g) powdered sugar
- 1 tsp vanilla extract
- ½ cup (50g) ground pistachios

Instructions

1. **Prepare the Cake:**
   - Preheat the oven to 350°F (175°C). Grease and line two 9-inch (23cm) round cake pans.
   - In a bowl, whisk together flour, baking powder, and salt.
   - In a large bowl, beat the butter and sugar until light and fluffy. Add eggs one at a time, mixing well after each addition. Stir in vanilla extract.
   - Gradually add the dry ingredients alternating with milk, mixing until smooth. Fold in the chopped pistachios.
   - Divide the batter between the pans and bake for 25–30 minutes or until a toothpick comes out clean. Let the cakes cool completely.
2. **Prepare the Frosting:**
   - Whip the heavy cream with powdered sugar and vanilla extract until stiff peaks form. Gently fold in the ground pistachios.
3. **Assemble the Cake:**

- Layer the cakes, spreading pistachio frosting between each layer. Frost the top and sides of the cake with the remaining frosting. Garnish with chopped pistachios.

Vanilla Lemon Poppy Seed Cake

Ingredients

For the Cake:

- 2 ½ cups (310g) all-purpose flour
- 1 ½ tsp baking powder
- ¼ tsp salt
- 1 cup (230g) unsalted butter, softened
- 1 ½ cups (300g) granulated sugar
- 3 large eggs
- 1 tsp vanilla extract
- 1 cup (240ml) milk
- Zest of 2 lemons
- 2 tbsp poppy seeds

For the Frosting:

- 2 cups (480ml) heavy whipping cream
- ½ cup (50g) powdered sugar
- 1 tsp vanilla extract
- 2 tbsp lemon juice
- Lemon zest for garnish

Instructions

1. **Prepare the Cake:**
    - Preheat the oven to 350°F (175°C). Grease and line two 9-inch (23cm) round cake pans.
    - In a bowl, whisk together flour, baking powder, and salt.
    - In a large bowl, beat the butter and sugar until light and fluffy. Add eggs one at a time, mixing well after each addition. Stir in vanilla extract.
    - Gradually add the dry ingredients alternating with milk, mixing until smooth. Fold in lemon zest and poppy seeds.
    - Divide the batter between the pans and bake for 25–30 minutes or until a toothpick comes out clean. Let the cakes cool completely.
2. **Prepare the Frosting:**
    - Whip the heavy cream with powdered sugar, vanilla extract, and lemon juice until stiff peaks form.
3. **Assemble the Cake:**

- Layer the cakes, spreading lemon poppy seed frosting between each layer. Garnish with lemon zest.

Vanilla Fudge Marble Cake

Ingredients

For the Cake:

- 2 ½ cups (310g) all-purpose flour
- 1 ½ tsp baking powder
- ¼ tsp salt
- 1 cup (230g) unsalted butter, softened
- 1 ½ cups (300g) granulated sugar
- 3 large eggs
- 1 tsp vanilla extract
- 1 cup (240ml) milk
- ½ cup (50g) cocoa powder
- ½ cup (100g) fudge sauce

For the Frosting:

- 2 cups (480ml) heavy whipping cream
- ½ cup (50g) powdered sugar
- 1 tsp vanilla extract

Instructions

1. **Prepare the Cake:**
    - Preheat the oven to 350°F (175°C). Grease and line two 9-inch (23cm) round cake pans.
    - In a bowl, whisk together flour, baking powder, and salt.
    - In a large bowl, beat the butter and sugar until light and fluffy. Add eggs one at a time, mixing well. Stir in vanilla extract.
    - Divide the batter into two parts. Add cocoa powder to one part, then alternate spoonfuls of the two batters into the pans. Swirl with a knife to create a marble effect.
    - Bake for 25–30 minutes or until a toothpick comes out clean. Let the cakes cool completely.
2. **Prepare the Frosting:**
    - Whip the heavy cream with powdered sugar and vanilla extract until stiff peaks form.
3. **Assemble the Cake:**

- Layer the cakes, spreading frosting between each layer. Drizzle fudge sauce over the top and garnish with chocolate shavings.

Vanilla Red Velvet Cake

Ingredients

For the Cake:

- 2 ½ cups (310g) all-purpose flour
- 1 ½ tsp baking powder
- ¼ tsp salt
- 1 cup (230g) unsalted butter, softened
- 1 ½ cups (300g) granulated sugar
- 3 large eggs
- 1 tsp vanilla extract
- 1 cup (240ml) buttermilk
- 2 tbsp red food coloring
- 1 tbsp cocoa powder

For the Frosting:

- 2 cups (480ml) heavy whipping cream
- ½ cup (50g) powdered sugar
- 1 tsp vanilla extract
- 2 tbsp cream cheese, softened

Instructions

1. **Prepare the Cake:**
   - Preheat the oven to 350°F (175°C). Grease and line two 9-inch (23cm) round cake pans.
   - In a bowl, whisk together flour, baking powder, and salt.
   - In a large bowl, beat the butter and sugar until light and fluffy. Add eggs one at a time, mixing well. Stir in vanilla extract.
   - Gradually add the dry ingredients alternating with buttermilk, mixing until smooth. Stir in red food coloring and cocoa powder.
   - Divide the batter between the pans and bake for 25–30 minutes or until a toothpick comes out clean. Let the cakes cool completely.
2. **Prepare the Frosting:**
   - Whip the heavy cream with powdered sugar, vanilla extract, and cream cheese until stiff peaks form.
3. **Assemble the Cake:**

- Layer the cakes, spreading cream cheese frosting between each layer. Frost the top and sides of the cake.

Vanilla Buttercream and Fruit Tart Cake

Ingredients

For the Cake:

- 2 ½ cups (310g) all-purpose flour
- 1 ½ tsp baking powder
- ¼ tsp salt
- 1 cup (230g) unsalted butter, softened
- 1 ½ cups (300g) granulated sugar
- 3 large eggs
- 1 tsp vanilla extract
- 1 cup (240ml) milk

For the Frosting:

- 2 cups (480ml) heavy whipping cream
- ½ cup (50g) powdered sugar
- 1 tsp vanilla extract
- Assorted fresh fruits (berries, kiwi, etc.)

Instructions

1. **Prepare the Cake:**
    - Preheat the oven to 350°F (175°C). Grease and line two 9-inch (23cm) round cake pans.
    - In a bowl, whisk together flour, baking powder, and salt.
    - In a large bowl, beat the butter and sugar until light and fluffy. Add eggs one at a time, mixing well. Stir in vanilla extract.
    - Gradually add the dry ingredients alternating with milk, mixing until smooth.
    - Divide the batter between the pans and bake for 25–30 minutes or until a toothpick comes out clean. Let the cakes cool completely.
2. **Prepare the Frosting:**
    - Whip the heavy cream with powdered sugar and vanilla extract until stiff peaks form.
3. **Assemble the Cake:**
    - Layer the cakes, spreading buttercream between each layer. Top the cake with fresh fruits and drizzle with honey if desired.

Vanilla Toffee Crunch Cake

Ingredients

For the Cake:

- 2 ½ cups (310g) all-purpose flour
- 1 ½ tsp baking powder
- ¼ tsp salt
- 1 cup (230g) unsalted butter, softened
- 1 ½ cups (300g) granulated sugar
- 3 large eggs
- 1 tsp vanilla extract
- 1 cup (240ml) milk
- ½ cup (100g) toffee bits

For the Frosting:

- 2 cups (480ml) heavy whipping cream
- ½ cup (50g) powdered sugar
- 1 tsp vanilla extract
- ½ cup (50g) toffee bits for garnish

Instructions

1. **Prepare the Cake:**
    - Preheat the oven to 350°F (175°C). Grease and line two 9-inch (23cm) round cake pans.
    - In a bowl, whisk together flour, baking powder, and salt.
    - In a large bowl, beat the butter and sugar until light and fluffy. Add eggs one at a time, mixing well. Stir in vanilla extract.
    - Gradually add the dry ingredients alternating with milk, mixing until smooth. Stir in toffee bits.
    - Divide the batter between the pans and bake for 25–30 minutes or until a toothpick comes out clean. Let the cakes cool completely.
2. **Prepare the Frosting:**
    - Whip the heavy cream with powdered sugar and vanilla extract until stiff peaks form.
3. **Assemble the Cake:**
    - Layer the cakes, spreading frosting between each layer. Frost the top and sides of the cake and sprinkle with toffee bits.

Vanilla with Caramelized Banana Cake

Ingredients

For the Cake:

- 2 ½ cups (310g) all-purpose flour
- 1 ½ tsp baking powder
- ¼ tsp salt
- 1 cup (230g) unsalted butter, softened
- 1 ½ cups (300g) granulated sugar
- 3 large eggs
- 1 tsp vanilla extract
- 1 cup (240ml) mashed ripe bananas

For the Caramelized Bananas:

- 2 ripe bananas, sliced
- 2 tbsp butter
- ¼ cup (50g) brown sugar
- 1 tsp vanilla extract

For the Frosting:

- 2 cups (480ml) heavy whipping cream
- ½ cup (50g) powdered sugar
- 1 tsp vanilla extract

Instructions

1. **Prepare the Cake:**
   - Preheat the oven to 350°F (175°C). Grease and line two 9-inch (23cm) round cake pans.
   - In a bowl, whisk together flour, baking powder, and salt.
   - In a large bowl, beat the butter and sugar until light and fluffy. Add eggs one at a time, mixing well. Stir in vanilla extract.
   - Gradually add the dry ingredients, alternating with mashed bananas, mixing until smooth.
   - Divide the batter between the pans and bake for 25–30 minutes or until a toothpick comes out clean. Let the cakes cool completely.
2. **Caramelize the Bananas:**

- In a skillet, melt butter over medium heat. Add banana slices and brown sugar, cooking for 3-4 minutes until caramelized. Stir in vanilla extract and remove from heat.
3. **Prepare the Frosting:**
    - Whip the heavy cream with powdered sugar and vanilla extract until stiff peaks form.
4. **Assemble the Cake:**
    - Layer the cakes, spreading frosting between each layer. Top with caramelized bananas and additional frosting.

Vanilla and White Chocolate Truffle Cake

Ingredients

For the Cake:

- 2 ½ cups (310g) all-purpose flour
- 1 ½ tsp baking powder
- ¼ tsp salt
- 1 cup (230g) unsalted butter, softened
- 1 ½ cups (300g) granulated sugar
- 3 large eggs
- 1 tsp vanilla extract
- 1 cup (240ml) milk
- ½ cup (90g) white chocolate chips

For the White Chocolate Truffle Filling:

- 1 cup (240ml) heavy cream
- 8 oz (225g) white chocolate, chopped

For the Frosting:

- 2 cups (480ml) heavy whipping cream
- ½ cup (50g) powdered sugar
- 1 tsp vanilla extract

Instructions

1. **Prepare the Cake:**
   - Preheat the oven to 350°F (175°C). Grease and line two 9-inch (23cm) round cake pans.
   - In a bowl, whisk together flour, baking powder, and salt.
   - In a large bowl, beat the butter and sugar until light and fluffy. Add eggs one at a time, mixing well. Stir in vanilla extract.
   - Gradually add the dry ingredients alternating with milk, mixing until smooth. Fold in white chocolate chips.
   - Divide the batter between the pans and bake for 25–30 minutes or until a toothpick comes out clean. Let the cakes cool completely.
2. **Prepare the White Chocolate Truffle Filling:**

- In a saucepan, heat heavy cream until just simmering. Pour over chopped white chocolate and let it sit for 2-3 minutes. Stir until smooth and set aside to cool.
3. **Prepare the Frosting:**
    - Whip the heavy cream with powdered sugar and vanilla extract until stiff peaks form.
4. **Assemble the Cake:**
    - Layer the cakes, spreading white chocolate truffle filling between each layer. Frost the top and sides of the cake with whipped cream.

Vanilla Maple Bacon Cake

Ingredients

For the Cake:

- 2 ½ cups (310g) all-purpose flour
- 1 ½ tsp baking powder
- ¼ tsp salt
- 1 cup (230g) unsalted butter, softened
- 1 ½ cups (300g) granulated sugar
- 3 large eggs
- 1 tsp vanilla extract
- 1 cup (240ml) milk
- ½ cup (100g) maple syrup

For the Bacon:

- 6 slices of bacon, cooked and crumbled

For the Frosting:

- 2 cups (480ml) heavy whipping cream
- ½ cup (50g) powdered sugar
- 1 tsp vanilla extract
- ¼ cup (60ml) maple syrup

Instructions

1. **Prepare the Cake:**
    - Preheat the oven to 350°F (175°C). Grease and line two 9-inch (23cm) round cake pans.
    - In a bowl, whisk together flour, baking powder, and salt.
    - In a large bowl, beat the butter and sugar until light and fluffy. Add eggs one at a time, mixing well. Stir in vanilla extract and maple syrup.
    - Gradually add the dry ingredients alternating with milk, mixing until smooth.
    - Divide the batter between the pans and bake for 25–30 minutes or until a toothpick comes out clean. Let the cakes cool completely.
2. **Prepare the Frosting:**

- Whip the heavy cream with powdered sugar, vanilla extract, and maple syrup until stiff peaks form.
3. **Assemble the Cake:**
    - Layer the cakes, spreading frosting between each layer. Top with crumbled bacon and additional frosting.

Vanilla and Cherry Cheesecake Cake

Ingredients

For the Cake:

- 2 ½ cups (310g) all-purpose flour
- 1 ½ tsp baking powder
- ¼ tsp salt
- 1 cup (230g) unsalted butter, softened
- 1 ½ cups (300g) granulated sugar
- 3 large eggs
- 1 tsp vanilla extract
- 1 cup (240ml) milk

For the Cheesecake Layer:

- 8 oz (225g) cream cheese, softened
- ½ cup (100g) granulated sugar
- 1 large egg
- 1 tsp vanilla extract

For the Frosting:

- 2 cups (480ml) heavy whipping cream
- ½ cup (50g) powdered sugar
- 1 tsp vanilla extract

For the Cherry Topping:

- 1 cup (250g) fresh cherries, pitted and halved

Instructions

1. **Prepare the Cake:**
   - Preheat the oven to 350°F (175°C). Grease and line two 9-inch (23cm) round cake pans.
   - In a bowl, whisk together flour, baking powder, and salt.
   - In a large bowl, beat the butter and sugar until light and fluffy. Add eggs one at a time, mixing well. Stir in vanilla extract.
   - Gradually add the dry ingredients alternating with milk, mixing until smooth. Divide the batter between the pans.

2. **Prepare the Cheesecake Layer:**
     - In a bowl, beat cream cheese and sugar until smooth. Add egg and vanilla extract, mixing until combined. Pour over the cake batter.
3. **Prepare the Frosting:**
     - Whip the heavy cream with powdered sugar and vanilla extract until stiff peaks form.
4. **Assemble the Cake:**
     - After baking, let the cakes cool completely. Layer them, spreading frosting and topping with fresh cherries.

Vanilla Cream Puff Swirl Cake

Ingredients

For the Cake:

- 2 ½ cups (310g) all-purpose flour
- 1 ½ tsp baking powder
- ¼ tsp salt
- 1 cup (230g) unsalted butter, softened
- 1 ½ cups (300g) granulated sugar
- 3 large eggs
- 1 tsp vanilla extract
- 1 cup (240ml) milk

For the Cream Puff Swirl:

- 1 cup (240ml) water
- ½ cup (115g) unsalted butter
- 1 cup (120g) all-purpose flour
- 4 large eggs
- ½ tsp vanilla extract
- 1 ½ cups (360ml) heavy cream
- ¼ cup (30g) powdered sugar

Instructions

1. **Prepare the Cake:**
    - Preheat the oven to 350°F (175°C). Grease and line two 9-inch (23cm) round cake pans.
    - In a bowl, whisk together flour, baking powder, and salt.
    - In a large bowl, beat the butter and sugar until light and fluffy. Add eggs one at a time, mixing well. Stir in vanilla extract.
    - Gradually add the dry ingredients alternating with milk, mixing until smooth. Divide the batter between the pans and bake for 25–30 minutes or until a toothpick comes out clean. Let the cakes cool completely.
2. **Prepare the Cream Puff Swirl:**
    - In a saucepan, bring water and butter to a boil. Add flour and stir vigorously until the mixture forms a ball. Remove from heat and let cool slightly.

- Add eggs one at a time, stirring until smooth after each addition. Stir in vanilla extract.
    - Drop spoonfuls of the cream puff batter in a spiral pattern on a parchment-lined baking sheet.
    - Bake at 350°F (175°C) for 20–25 minutes until golden brown. Allow to cool.
3. **Prepare the Frosting:**
    - Whip the heavy cream with powdered sugar until stiff peaks form.
4. **Assemble the Cake:**
    - Layer the cakes with whipped cream and place the cream puff swirls on top. Garnish with additional cream if desired.

Vanilla Fig and Almond Cake

Ingredients

For the Cake:

- 2 ½ cups (310g) all-purpose flour
- 1 ½ tsp baking powder
- ¼ tsp salt
- 1 cup (230g) unsalted butter, softened
- 1 ½ cups (300g) granulated sugar
- 3 large eggs
- 1 tsp vanilla extract
- 1 cup (240ml) milk
- 1 cup (150g) chopped dried figs
- ½ cup (50g) ground almonds

For the Frosting:

- 2 cups (480ml) heavy whipping cream
- ½ cup (50g) powdered sugar
- 1 tsp vanilla extract

Instructions

1. **Prepare the Cake:**
    - Preheat the oven to 350°F (175°C). Grease and line two 9-inch (23cm) round cake pans.
    - In a bowl, whisk together flour, baking powder, salt, and ground almonds.
    - In a large bowl, beat the butter and sugar until light and fluffy. Add eggs one at a time, mixing well. Stir in vanilla extract.
    - Gradually add the dry ingredients alternating with milk, mixing until smooth. Fold in chopped figs.
    - Divide the batter between the pans and bake for 25–30 minutes or until a toothpick comes out clean. Let the cakes cool completely.
2. **Prepare the Frosting:**
    - Whip the heavy cream with powdered sugar and vanilla extract until stiff peaks form.
3. **Assemble the Cake:**
    - Layer the cakes, spreading frosting between each layer. Frost the top and sides of the cake.

Vanilla Pineapple Coconut Cake

Ingredients

For the Cake:

- 2 ½ cups (310g) all-purpose flour
- 1 ½ tsp baking powder
- ¼ tsp salt
- 1 cup (230g) unsalted butter, softened
- 1 ½ cups (300g) granulated sugar
- 3 large eggs
- 1 tsp vanilla extract
- 1 cup (240ml) milk
- 1 cup (240g) crushed pineapple, drained
- 1 cup (90g) shredded coconut

For the Frosting:

- 2 cups (480ml) heavy whipping cream
- ½ cup (50g) powdered sugar
- 1 tsp vanilla extract
- ½ cup (40g) shredded coconut for garnish

Instructions

1. **Prepare the Cake:**
    - Preheat the oven to 350°F (175°C). Grease and line two 9-inch (23cm) round cake pans.
    - In a bowl, whisk together flour, baking powder, and salt.
    - In a large bowl, beat the butter and sugar until light and fluffy. Add eggs one at a time, mixing well. Stir in vanilla extract.
    - Gradually add the dry ingredients alternating with milk, mixing until smooth. Fold in crushed pineapple and shredded coconut.
    - Divide the batter between the pans and bake for 25–30 minutes or until a toothpick comes out clean. Let the cakes cool completely.
2. **Prepare the Frosting:**
    - Whip the heavy cream with powdered sugar and vanilla extract until stiff peaks form.
3. **Assemble the Cake:**

- Layer the cakes, spreading frosting between each layer. Frost the top and sides of the cake and sprinkle with shredded coconut.

Vanilla Blackberry Jam Cake

Ingredients

For the Cake:

- 2 ½ cups (310g) all-purpose flour
- 1 ½ tsp baking powder
- ¼ tsp salt
- 1 cup (230g) unsalted butter, softened
- 1 ½ cups (300g) granulated sugar
- 3 large eggs
- 1 tsp vanilla extract
- 1 cup (240ml) milk
- ¾ cup (200g) blackberry jam

For the Frosting:

- 2 cups (480ml) heavy whipping cream
- ½ cup (50g) powdered sugar
- 1 tsp vanilla extract

Instructions

1. **Prepare the Cake:**
    - Preheat the oven to 350°F (175°C). Grease and line two 9-inch (23cm) round cake pans.
    - In a bowl, whisk together flour, baking powder, and salt.
    - In a large bowl, beat the butter and sugar until light and fluffy. Add eggs one at a time, mixing well. Stir in vanilla extract.
    - Gradually add the dry ingredients alternating with milk, mixing until smooth. Fold in blackberry jam.
    - Divide the batter between the pans and bake for 25–30 minutes or until a toothpick comes out clean. Let the cakes cool completely.
2. **Prepare the Frosting:**
    - Whip the heavy cream with powdered sugar and vanilla extract until stiff peaks form.
3. **Assemble the Cake:**
    - Layer the cakes, spreading frosting between each layer. Frost the top and sides of the cake.

Vanilla Custard Layer Cake

Ingredients

For the Cake:

- 2 ½ cups (310g) all-purpose flour
- 1 ½ tsp baking powder
- ¼ tsp salt
- 1 cup (230g) unsalted butter, softened
- 1 ½ cups (300g) granulated sugar
- 3 large eggs
- 1 tsp vanilla extract
- 1 cup (240ml) milk

For the Custard Filling:

- 1 ½ cups (360ml) whole milk
- 1/3 cup (65g) granulated sugar
- 3 large egg yolks
- 2 tbsp cornstarch
- 1 tsp vanilla extract

For the Frosting:

- 2 cups (480ml) heavy whipping cream
- ½ cup (50g) powdered sugar
- 1 tsp vanilla extract

Instructions

1. **Prepare the Cake:**
    - Preheat the oven to 350°F (175°C). Grease and line two 9-inch (23cm) round cake pans.
    - In a bowl, whisk together flour, baking powder, and salt.
    - In a large bowl, beat the butter and sugar until light and fluffy. Add eggs one at a time, mixing well. Stir in vanilla extract.
    - Gradually add the dry ingredients alternating with milk, mixing until smooth. Divide the batter between the pans and bake for 25–30 minutes or until a toothpick comes out clean. Let the cakes cool completely.
2. **Prepare the Custard Filling:**

- In a saucepan, combine milk and sugar. In a separate bowl, whisk egg yolks and cornstarch until smooth. Gradually add hot milk to the egg mixture, whisking constantly. Return to heat and cook until thickened, about 3-5 minutes. Remove from heat and stir in vanilla extract. Allow to cool completely.
3. **Prepare the Frosting:**
    - Whip the heavy cream with powdered sugar and vanilla extract until stiff peaks form.
4. **Assemble the Cake:**
    - Layer the cakes, spreading custard filling between each layer. Frost the top and sides of the cake with whipped cream.

www.ingramcontent.com/pod-product-compliance
Lightning Source LLC
LaVergne TN
LVHW081320060526
838201LV00055B/2386